SKIN TAX

For my parents,
Felix & Lydia
with love, respect, & gratitude
siempre.

Skin Tax

TIM Z. HERNANDEZ

Foreword by Juan Felipe Herrera

Great Valley Books

Heyday Books, Berkeley, California

Library of Congress Cataloging-in-Publication Data

Hernandez, Tim Z.
  Skin tax / Tim Z. Hernandez ; foreword by Juan Felipe Herrera.
    p. cm.
  "Great Valley books."
  ISBN 1-890771-93-7 (pbk. : alk. paper)
  1. Young men—Poetry. 2. Masculinity—Poetry. I. Title.
  PS3608.E768S58 2004
  811'.6--dc22

                                                  2004015695

Book design by Rebecca LeGates
Printing and Binding: Bang Printing, Brainerd, MN

Orders, inquiries, and correspondence should be addressed to:
      Heyday Books
      P.O. Box 9145, Berkeley, CA 94709
      (510) 549-3564, Fax (510) 549-1889
      www.heydaybooks.com

Printed in the United States of America

10 9 8 7 6 5 4 3 2 1

CONTENTS

DEATH & BLOSSOMS

ACKNOWLEDGMENTS

Abrazos to the following for their endless support: My three pillars—the Hernandez, Morones, and Sevilla families. A deep bow of respect to Juan Felipe Herrera & Margarita Luna Robles for kundalini guidance, the Zuniga Family, Michael Roberts, Adolfo Guzman Lopez, Bob Warkentin, David Herrera, Estela Sue, the Chicano Writers & Artists Association, the Rogue Festival Committee, Kevin Chen & the Intersection for the Arts staff, the California Council for the Humanities, the San Francisco Foundation, Linda Watanabe McFerrin, Kevin Killian, Reginald Lockett, & the Heyday staff. Embraces to my extended family: Mike, Devoya, Erasmo, Ramiro, & the rest of the artistas up from the fields of everywhere, and finally—Dayanna, singer/healer to whom I owe the heart & guts of this book. *Namaste!*

I am grateful to the following publications for including some of the poems in this book: "Madness Flows Through," *Mosaic Voices;* "Enter Madrugada," "Elegy For C-Dog," *Flies, Cockroaches, & Poets;* "I Arrive Late," *The Ram's Tale;* and "I've Worn That Feminine Skin," *Jambalaya.*

FORE-WORD FLOW

This is one river:

one river of words, one embrace, one spoken song in the
key of Rumi, Machado and Hafiz wearing dandelions on the
cuffs, asphalt on the belt, one inner diary, going in and out, a
reverie, an entrance, an exit, a mantra shouting out death-
birth-emptiness, bliss, body, being, mama-womb-goddess-
consort to Mex-Siddhartha, to the spoken poetry-heart with
a hole, a wound, a pause, a liminal Big Bang where all is
manifold, "a warm familiar sack of membrane," call it
docile-ooze, wine-colored, soft, silken, cushion, a gown, an
embryonic universe of love-stuff-mind-dust, jelly, yes, the
spoken-poem speaks of jelly, a fem-jelly, the images rush and
burst and churn and turn, a delicate shimmy between gen-
der codes and male assigned Gestapo orientations, a nuance,
it is recast here, after four decades of politico-poesy move-
ments, a delicate tidal tear of salt and scents and blood and
sniff and smooch, upper-heavens, even Dante appears,
above, middle and below, this tripartite discourse of coursing
intercourse, better say "the chain-smoking engine of flesh,"
repeat chain, repeat engine, repeat flesh as the spoken-heart
here says, a "glutton of a Body Self," what it is, then, this
Vortex of Consumptions, agglutinations, coagulations, pene-
trations, amalgamations, invasions, meat, notice this too, the
meat we eat, the meat we lay, the meat we say, the meat we
beat, the meat that we meet, cawing, flapping, inside, out-
side, let's move this mobius shell—there are no boundaries,

no true and authentic borders, or divisions in the one river, no absolutes carved into finite systems of being or identity or proclamation, or essence, maybe this is Rabelais destroyed in the forlorn broken shack highways of the San Joaquin Valley, Yevtushenko at Fresno Station speaking vulgar Volga in Chicano nakedness, impure syrups, lavas, nasty persimmons, a questionable garden on the mustache, the pubic flora, dirty meditations, that is more accurate, a neo-Tibetan Lama with Lust Loss Sutras, creams, aloes and kisses, necks and foolishness, what happened to ideology, to caesurae, to raucous religion and violent vexed views and preposterous puny poetic positions against the State, it is all "gurgling" now, it is all "putty dumb" liquor-dipped skin, listen to that, feel that, be that, is-that, no Foucault is necessary in this textual positivist pyscho-pump of excretions and cellular disintegrations, a Barrio Barthes of the Latino body signifying, but there is no barrio, O yes, the skin, the skin-words, everywhere, the permeability of being and cosmos and body and transgender and mind, this is the marinade in the one river, this is what the mass is, the culture-cube, this is what the masses are, the global mud of power, that is, the mass of time and thought and desire, permeable, made of fish-eye holes, better yet, emptiness and compassion, nothing is focused, by the way, get this, *nothing is clear,* we live in a hemorrhage with a pencil, we are in a state of blurred categories and tender touches, all this is a subversive *manifesto* of Twenty-First Century Grammar, we are condemned to re-read, up close, like soft television, one arm into one thigh, going into one breast plate, if we can call it a plate, going into one "acoustic muscle," every thing is saying things, at "play" in the roomy river, out and about, fuzzy, wet, dangling, sobbing, a casserole, crumbling, of course all this feels like a raunchy Renaissance adoration, a footloose fiesta, a

gumbo gone akimbo, a Latino Kwakiutl potlatch ceremony
without the pot, or a Pietá, that is, who can truly hold Love
or God or Goddess on your arms, but, there are no capital
letters, no reified skin-tax, there is a father, yes, there is a
mother, yes, and there is a son, the first one, the first poem,
there are the skins where we begin, in a way, these are the
bounded figures we must deconstruct along the path even if
we you he she us them cry "Everything must go back to
how it was," isn't this what we all are saying, post 911, isn't
this how we really are, bent back, our metaphysics askew
into an intrinsic pessimism of progress, but the one river has
no beginning, no ending, this is all we know, no proper
grammar, so we go to the "lover's side," if we can call it
that, where the heat rises, so says this sexy exposé boy, he'll
call you a maricón, a queer, legs waxed and the melancholy
body-writing babble spills, a frothy Klimt talkin' Burroughs
jive, rouge street mini-novels, the lives of Lonely, the trans-
vestite, hustling in the barrio yards, C-Dog in a "cheap-ass"
hotel room, the lover's miscarriages in deep reds, his drunk-
en hallucinations, Little Joe blowin' his horns of maleness
and femininity, chile and onions, wallets and cherries, dusty
dichotomies, day-glo-memoria, cry-baby-destructions,
blushed herstories, shy-boy tellings, with his lips puffed open
and "black cloth over his eyes," hurry, the one river rolls fast,
it does not stop to take your name, it is boiling, steaming,
raging, mad in its Tejano tints and bare-shouldered har-
monies, I hear Ginsberg riffin' his music box and clanging his
Buddha bells, I hear Anaïs Nin smacking her lips ripping out
pages from her diary into confetti here, fore-word to Oscar
Zeta Acosta, the raw brown sex sixties buffalo of desire and
shame, fire and pain, with his cockroach poesy crackin,'
fore-word to '85's *Ya Vas, Carnal,* the first all-out gay Latino
chapbook of horny odes and manlove meditations, Tim

echoes these radical voicings, this age we know now, he laughs out of control, incisions, and hot bellies, oceans harmonica-rushing out of the heart, we go with this river, sharp and wise, blundering and symbolic, it is the Other Speaker, could it be, the "Monster Man," with the Ax, the tax without a tee, it is amazing, it is your karma if you believe in that stuff, our destiny, if you subscribe to that jive, our shrunken, "turtle-necked" will to power, our romancing heated viscera, Saguaro and shrapnel, the color of bougainvillea, global war, that is—your mighty skin-takers and destroyers—and war-givers, it is happening right now, jitterbuggin' across the softest part of your being live(s), across time, territory and generations of comfort—here, where lines, titles, spaces, images, names, remembrances, bodies, births, deaths, and naked desserts take us in, butter you up, so, you can taste this, you can love this, it is you, the skin, the tax "blasted shimmering holes into the night—the one river, dissolving the historical rant, the cultural reclamation trope and the hep haughty male staccato of suave social solutions; thirty-five years after Latino Floricanto Poetica flourished Tim enters naked, into a feminine stream if we can call it that, better yet, his poems abandon the macho monumentalism of his forerunners, he doesn't seek to build upon their "Raza Power" scaffoldings, he delves into the waters, formless........this first Tim Hernandez book of twenty-five pieces floating in four directions—a masterpiece without precedent.

Juan Felipe Herrera
Fresno Station, April 2004

SKIN TAX

I.

My story gets told in various ways:
a romance, a dirty joke, a war, a vacancy.
—Rumi

MAMA'S BOY

They say I'm a Mama's Boy
        like it's a bad thing, when all along
                I thought that's what a man was.
        They say my skin was made from goat's milk
                        & dandelions
                and that my eyes were plucked
                        from cherry blossoms in the
                                month of February

A Mama's Boy, they say,
        with hands too soft for picking
    legs thin as sprigs of mesquite
        They say my voice lacks
            the asphalt grit of courage, that I
                should work on it
                    and that my name is even too short
                                to call me by name,
                        and they're right

When they say
                I was born with a hole in my heart
                    the size of a tiny fish eye. They're right
                        when they shout Mama's Boy,
                                and poke at the tenderness
                                that is my back
claiming that my hair was quilted from a beggar's scarf
        and that my smile was strewn from tender husks of sugar cane,
                                        it's true—

Since I've fondled and groped at the inside
        of my mama's womb,

just a squirming confirmation
of father's lust,
I've been scheming ways to retreat to that
warm familiar sack of membrane
and love manifold

This is why
I lead with the docile nose of a house cat
speak my intentions
in raw doggerel utterances
from the stiff core of a loose taciturn tongue,
why I tweeze the nose hair clean
behind locked doors
using the reflection off surgical steel buck-knives
& limp toilet handles,
lather my jaw with baking powder and lava rock
skin tax
for the morning peel
Because I am soft,
zephyr soft
and teeming with secrets

I am the watermark of houses submerged
My whimpering howl a rivulet of what remains
from the hidden
tidal tears of men
Which is why
they do not lie when they say that
my feeble knees are the silken steel edges
of grandfather's worn plow discs
tease that my stomach is a sofa cushion
stuffed with the down of a thousand geese
and that my nipples are the fragile embroidery
of Victorian gowns

My words
they say, these boyish longings
do not pounce from the gut like

      alloy   drum   fire
         candy   wine   lingo

do not come on like

      razor   neck   nicks
        splashed   in allspice   fire

will not crowbar the ribcage
will not shoehorn the chunk boot
or adorn the rearview in

      deer   hoof   rabbit
     knuckle   luck charms

Instead, they are made from
sugar water & pomegranate lust
jelly for the dawn song
Warm rhythms for the doubtful eye &
the accusing heart

It is because of this,
they jab their crooked fingers in my face
and shout, *Mama's Boy!*
like it's a bad thing
when all along, you see,
I thought
that's what a Man was.

I'VE WORN THAT FEMININE SKIN

but you refused it—
called me a queer
said my affection with men bothered you,
said I held too long
that I cried too hard
that my hair should smell appropriately male,
said a man who smells of lavender & sage is no man at all

Wondered aloud about
why I must talk before sex
why I must talk during sex
why I must talk after sex
and still you wonder why men are such liars
ignorant & soulless
empty carcasses of
scar & bone

Truth is—we're born from lies
been nurtured on gun smoke and horse muscle
told grown men can hang
faked the courage of hunters & heroes
of righteous soldiers
erect & stoic in their stance

Our whole lives
we've aimed to reach you,
to keep still that image of us
to chop the logs that fuel the fire
so that we can tender our touch
—and it's been this way for a long time

But secretly, amongst the boys,
amongst the shadow-faced truckers and
          slick hot-rodders of gurgling grease
                    We revel in this lust
               We shit-talk 'round bonfires
          of our once thriving pasts,
          but we speak highly of you
               —build you up

                    This is why we refuse to bathe
                         To erase the scent
                    Why we leave the salt
                         To preserve the sex
                    Why we scratch our balls
                         To sniff our fingers
                                   reminding us
                              of when we entered heaven
                         through a hole in the thrust
                    of a woman's wings.

WE'VE BEEN AFRAID

to say these things for too long now—
    That we dream up lust at the sight of you,
        for fear of being called a pervert
            a dirty cock talkin' womanizer

                wo   men   eyes   her

        But I'm tired of this masquerade,
    tired of keeping these feelings to myself
    with no one to share the panorama with except
        the other *Self*
        I've created
        from necessity

        The chain-smoking engine of flesh
           Monster Man
           Glutton of a Body *Self*
           Paunch Stark
           Gut Guzzler
    of all the meat I have to speak of

    Alone we play images of you,
        Monster Man & I,
        each time enhancing
        the possibility of our odds
        emphasizing those things
        that make you
        woman fierce
        & edible

    But not this time,
        not in this poem!
            I want to send these crows cawing

flapping static
from the telephone wires of my hair
across mountains of men and plains
of men to be,
so that they can come clean
about the men they are
About the man
    inside the man,
    and
    the women they lust.

I want to speak of my lust:

When I catch you midriffed
sashimi smooth & silken
ballerina steppin' past

I imagine the tender meat
of your hips
the lathed ivory of mammoth tusks
where I grip animal grunting
against the bone of you

The triangle
flag of panty line
above the butt crack
spaghetti slung thong
of frankincense and smudge stack
embers of pubic blues

I want to sing my lust
harder than a preacher sings—
            Hallelujah!
    The hot *semilla* bread of your breasts
sprouting glacier teeth when days get cold and

excitement goes pimpling the skin—
Hallelujah!
The cups of black hair dipping across your face,
raven winged & perfumed to the plume—
Hallelujah!
My grease fire angel bird cooing glue
between us

I want to graffiti my lust
on all the walls ever erected
The crimson cave of mouth leading into you
where breath and drink sink down the throat
past two tonsils on a warm bed
of tongue

The foothills of thigh engulfing the valley
where irrigation leaks in furrows
A blossom
Then your fruit gets picked with these two hands

Because I've got needs! Damn,
I've got needs no pope or priest could redeem,
ideas that would incarcerate me
for a thousand lifetimes!

But there's nothing wrong with this,
it's what your body invokes,
it's the fire that ravishes the hillside,
goes clawing at the land
charring roots
spitting blue flames from brilliant gardens
churning creatures from hot houses
sending everything up in dark
clouds to cry rain
on next year's sprouts.

HOW UNUSUAL IT WOULD BE

if for one naked moment
I didn't conjure up
an X girl's face
to make the experience new again
to revive
the exhibitionist
   teenager in me,
of my junior college fervor &
                    legal drunk dick drive

Anywhere women gave themselves
to me I'd take it
               In their mother's kitchen bare-assed
               on island chopping blocks,
               where we dropped our jeans to the cool linoleum
               I plucked your panties and gave it to you
                    butcher bruise
               before your mom found you
                    hair back
                    crab-legging me into you
               My pimply ass flexing
                    churning curd from the smell of us—
               chowder cloud & clammy

Amidst the sour breath
   of peach guts
   on hot car hoods

Unlike the city, where two can fuck in alleyway depths,
   we gorge ourselves
   in true country fashion

Fetching leaves without blossoms
to scoop the sludge
that found its way into your bellybutton

I remember the Econo-Hotel
where your breasts like two
buoys kept me bobbing
in waves of billowing arches,
citing any man would die to lay you,
die to have your pretty primrose
lopped by his slung cutter

The desperate attempts
of spoiled girls
who'll do and say anything
to have their wants
Daddy's little girls

pouty puppies
wagging tail
panting pussy promises

I've heard them all before:

I'll suck you
Love you
Paint me nude
Make me yours

So, I did
and still do
In those moments
when my dick is there,

limp and turtle-necked
    in its simple skin
    and I am faced with the silence
    of a couple
    who have done and said it all,
    nothing pleases me more
    than a greedy tug at the fuse
    to spark
    to blow
    to ignite
    the memory;

Firm cream flora of sister peaks
Shriveled jagged prune buds
Registers of desire
Red syrup slop of lips
Hard denim thrusts of your impatience
The canyon of your crotch opening its

      slick   cod   orchid
        hot   liver   lava

Your hand
    taking my hand there
      taking my mouth there
        where you begged for me to bite down
          enough to break the skin
          Put them in, you said
          until I plunged all five in the
          honey of your hive
          wore its thick molasses
          like a thin glove

Cedar
    & cardamom rose
        to the empty and brutal night

    Oh yes, it was you woman—
        nasty pulp of persimmon.

I'D BE A LYING MAN

                    if I pretended
                    that your ass didn't make me
                    Imagine

                    pulling back that zipper
              peeling you out from rinds
                         digging you to core
          juice, seed,
                    and pulp

     sending the arms and fingers sprouting up toward clouds
              begging rain to come
     dousing out the fires from within
              earth's bones
              before earth jolts
              and comes a volcano of orgasm,
     enough to ignite the rim
              of the pacific coast
     and solder all the ocean
              to a standstill
     closing up the gaps between land
              dusting sea creatures
              in mid thrust
     blowing birds from sky
     forcing mountains from meditation

If I didn't tell you
          that my head conjures up scenarios
               fit for magazine racks and
                    late night television,

· 15 ·

If I said in a romantic tone
            that I could read you
                  that I could tug between
                              your legs like the pages of a book
                        lick the tips of my fingers and flip you
                                    chapter for chapter
                                    Enunciate the syllables
                                    Pronounce the pelvis
                                    Roll the thighs
                                    Tongue the tease
                                    Project the sex

If I said I could
            break the spine to bookmark
                        the orgasm for another time

      Would that make me a literal man
                  —with crates of literature stacked
                        and overflowing
                                    from the crotch?

II.

To touch my person to someone else is about as much as I can stand.
—Walt Whitman

Z IS THE SHAPE

Of your body
Tucked in
Slavering sleep
On summer cotton sheets
In a room where walls brag
Holes like chipped horns
On a matador's mantle.

I RUB MY HANDS

with your cream
cocoa butter & aloe
on my skin reminds me of the times
I've denied your love

In the supermarket
when your hand slips into the curve of my back pocket
       and you whisper kisses
       against the meat of my neck

       I pull away—
A man afraid of what message
affection might bring
What foolishness

if I leaned into you
and took honest love
anytime you wanted it
       What foolishness
if I nipped back at you
       with puckered lips
       like an infant gurgling
at the coo of his mother's voice

and a passerby catch me
       in love
       being lovely with you
          and your woman ways

Worse yet, another man
with wife in tow

spot me gurgling
      putty dumb

eyes aglow
and walk away thinking thoughts
of how foolish I appear
stripped down

by my lover's side
balls braided
at the flimsy tips of
thin fingers

How silly I'd appear
cutting loose at the sight of you
      'round every corner
      in every movie house

Romanced madly
pecking at your affection
      like a kitten clucks
      at its mother's tit

love glazed & lathered
      by you
and the hands that lotion
themselves with cocoa butter & aloe

     I reject your touch
and love you from where I stand
      because stepping closer
      would mean leaving this place

I have lived for a lifetime
have carved from
granite, soot,
                    & dirty skin

I deny myself
of the child I become
when sharing a meal
                    with you

spooning
hot soup into one another's
open mouth
I peer inside and wonder

        if the bed
of my tongue exposed
        looks as tender
and vulnerable as yours

If I am a man
then you will not see the inside
of my mouth
taking in anything

        by you or your giving spoon
in a crowded space
        where a passerby might stare,
think me hungry

I deny your love
        and pay the price nightly
Smother my skin
        in cocoa butter & aloe

slide fingers between fingers
    drowning calluses
    hand over hand
touching, whiffing deeply

        like a puppy burrowing
        into an inviting crotch
        gobbling at the warm scent
        of living

remembering the times
        I've denied myself publicly
        of your affection
for fear of a passerby

spotting me
in love
being lovely
with you
        and your woman ways.

YOUR SKIN

is the mahogany pulp of wet earth
        undulated by centuries of passionate exchanges;
soilcombing granitepounding rivertonguing windthrusting
        sunpenetrating soil

and I am buried to the shoulders with it
        The caramel mass of your thighs,
           the brandy molasses of your sagging plum womb

it reads like jagged graffiti
    etched in obsidian flint permanence.
        Since we danced barefoot

on the wooden keys of ribs, when my liver pleaded with me
        to swallow you in ferocious gulps,
      even then I desired your fingers strumming

the dense thickness of my hair with the
                raw wings of flamenco

Even then, I would have drowned
        my dreams in a gutter of ambition
just to press against you like the pages in a book

I would have cracked a lifetime of spines
        to inhale the worn familiarity of your breath
           breathing into me

the recipes of your hidden ancestral hearts.
Your skin
is a tobacco leaf hidden in the umber chasm

of the king's cellar over seven generations
It's potency, enough to send volcanoes gagging ash and lung
turning spring skies into black holes of desperation

Your ankles are the diligent masts of Magellan's ship
pivoting in the maelstrom of a fierce rumba squall
Every strand of hair on your head is a blade of *yerba buena*

curing the invisible bellyache of the atmosphere
Your hips, a thick cello yawning

against a bone orchestra of vertebrae
Your ears are the tender folds of an oyster
dipped in a sweet marinade

from the supple orgasm of honeybees,
their buzz resonates on the tip of my tongue
each time I go whispering desire

Forget what they say—
your skin is a talking drum stretched with jaguar hide
banging song into the Amazon night

Your brows are a braided string of bougainvilleas
clawing above the wavering shutters of two open windows
which hide and expose

what cooks in the kitchen kiln. The warm loaf of your breasts
strings an aromatic ribbon from the blue flame
of your hearth

and I follow that ribbon,
riding on the grand crescendo
of a violin.

I ARRIVE LATE

you are on your back
wrapped in a paper gown

> your clothes lie limp
> in bundles beside you

your toenails are chipped
and ridged like candy apples

> in the white white
> loneliness of waiting

you remain still,
shining like a nickel

> tucked beneath the icebox.
> I search for your face

hidden beneath the mass of forearm
and thick tassels of your hair.

> A gauze panty dowsed in blood sticks
> to the cold linoleum floor and

tears have fallen everywhere.
I want to cradle you

> place your head in my lap and strum
> the tufts of wet strands

away from your mouth, but I am afraid
affection is what brought us here.

      Your hand reaches out and lifts
      a sad finger pointing

down beneath my seat
where you placed a small plastic cup

      for me to consider.
      I lean over to look and must focus my eyes:

a violet wad
of bulbous flesh.

      This, you say, *is my fault,*
      my body hates me.

I want to speak but breath has abandoned me.
The smell of latex unfurls over the silence

      until both become unbearable.
      In a bolt of warmth my stomach contracts

to hold itself,
causing the hair on my arm to lift

      as if in defiance of
      my own skin.

III.

I am my face in the wind, against the wind,
and I am the wind that strikes my face.
—Eduardo Galeano

IT STARTED

in the living room
with talk of bills
baby names
        and lust.

You said my job at the shop didn't pay enough,
that I should check the classifieds for something
                    worth calling a job.
        You Bitch! I said
        and in maelstrom tongue
    cussed your name with every last
            heap of exhaust burning in my bones,
        said, *Bitch!*
            again because it hurt the first time

Because insult is a switchblade that carves
            the hot scar of pride,
        and damned if I was going to let you
                    tear me down like that! Damn you
        for slapping me slack-jawed with my own cupped hand
        for two-timing my trust
        with that manipulation mascara
        snake slithering down your eyes
                into my concrete heart
And you froze stiff
anchored down with fear
        Not of my words
        but of the wolves I kept
            on choke chains and gun powder,
        until the baby came poking out
        from behind the door,

terrified and naïve
So we took it in the room
as good parents do

Swinging machetes from beneath our breath
cussing long currents of curare & cud
Blast the terrifying rhythm
of grunt & chop
tug & heave
to call the shots
to massacre the body
of our disease
Remember?

How the baby cried from behind the slamming door
Windows stuttering out
like blackbirds from telephone wires
Until we found her sprawled amongst
plastic dolls and stuffed puppies
Princess of her fantasy family
whimpering   recluse

make
believe

tantrum.

THE GUITAR

cracked open
like an alligator's egg

its strings frayed
loose tendons dangling

from the acoustic muscle
strumming its last chord

against the splintered bone
of fingers.

THE CAJON'S FACE

opened
like a botched c-section

spitting shards of wooden teeth
from entrails & black fire

with broken gobs of sobbing rhythm
spilling from its empty womb

THE LIVING ROOM

still stinks like fish
from when I chucked
the tuna casserole across the kitchen

the teal dish
dipped and dug a hole
splintering filet

in stucco
chalk chunks and mayo
fish grease and stud swell

dicing the onion grout
the wall boomed and
spit teeth of cheap ceramic

bitterness & jealousy in gobs
of pissed dinnerware and
seafood rage.

It was about you
    saying yes to men
        saying yes to anything I feared;

your tradition of greeting
        with a true kiss
        was simple indulgence to me

growing up on handshakes and
                    shoulder pummels
        I only touched a face for sexual gain

or simple lust
but never in the pure act
of public affection—never.

Your language was a game
the other kids played without me
was a code I couldn't break

a code my parents used to plot
punishments
is the one cheek elders find irresistible to pinch.

Your language is the high school crush
that laughed at my attempts,
sent me scampering home in an embarrassed rage

only to approach me years later
in a bar where I'd deny you publicly
my heart still tapping an SOS for yours.

Was about how many wrongs it took to admit it
how many rights I've been
to apply the pressure

to wield the key that turns the day on
sets the temperature for the year
—like this rage was born

from the tenderness of my past
and in that sudden jolt of fear
empty-handed

I make what I've got
of four knuckles, flint,
and a heart full of fire

yank love from its thriving nest and
fling it against the wall
where it lies writhing in agony—

like a dolphin crumbling
in sunlight.

I HEARD MY FATHER

> call my mom a Bitch once
> —and swore I'd never do the same.

But when the head quakes with a child's desperation
> the ribs bow out and
> the tongue can't hide
> the mind-swell stirring
> dagger words come unannounced
> > to push   to scare
> > > to kill   the spirit

relentless as a boy
prodding roosters with a pellet gun.

> Yes,
I've swatted that boy across the face
for disrespecting
the love of a woman
> but even his own father was a child
> who ached
> when the ol' man smacked the Maker
> toothless
> left her wry
> smiling in family portraits
with her back to the moon
and a grin that hinted
> of a loss she'd never gain—
> > never stopped him from using the name.

> Yes,
I've placed that boy on my knee and spoke gently to him
against the nightlight glow

where father and son
   cultivate the heart muscle
   into a bold & fearless thump
Whispering stories in the rugged embrace
   of a man's jagged jaw
   against the suppleness of a boy's cheek,
   I acted out
the seven small men AND
   the compassionate princess
    spread my arms and held their little heads
    against my bosom
   swore my gratitude,
  my loyalty to the village,
    until his eyes rolled and shut me out.

 Yes,
I've done away with privileges and playtime
   drew up a list of chores and put his ungrateful ass to work
Plucking weeds from the spring garden,
Shoveling shit with sprigs & short hoe,
Dusting webs from high corners,
Scrubbing bowls,
Plunging back ups,
Scraping gum
   from beneath the table.
   No time for a summer dip,
    or a brewing bath
     in winter, hell no!
   This time you'll pay—
    you'll pay until the house gets cleaned
     and your fingers worn
     holes to the soul son—
      Everything must be replaced! I cried—
      Everything must go back to how it was!

DEATH & BLOSSOMS

Peaches—once touched
they leave you
with a soft coat
of thorns to remember them by.

I PISSED ON LITTLE RICKY

because the guys dared me to.
          He was in the sandbox hunched over

plowing his Tonka truck through tiny dunes when
          Pelon, his big brother, left him there to get more toys.

I had to go pee real bad and one of the guys blurted,
          I dare you to piss on him! So, I did,

impulsively spraying on his powder brown hair.
          A fiery gush of yellow went stinging down his face,

drowning his soft shoulders, scalding his little eyes,
          and we ran.

Behind us, his tiny lungs exhausted
          every bit of air they held

out into the vacant valley sky
          —and we laughed.

Days later, while at school, a crop duster blew past our playground,
          its over-spray stung my face like a hornet's dagger,

unraveling a ribbon of blood that clung
          from my nose and wrapped around me,

ending in a fancy knot.

ELEGY FOR C-DOG

I.

Maybe it was me
when pops went down
his head against the concrete,
          it made a swoosh sound like when
     mom used to split peaches
               with her bare thumbnails.

And maybe it was me
          who cracked that iron mallet to the back of his oily skull
     for making mom & me wait up all these years
               for coming home drunk off his feet and never giving a shit
                    about what family means
                         or son means
                         or love means.

I wish it was me
               who could take the rap for dropping his ass
     to that stiff darkness for every Christmas that passed without
                    so much as a gift, or even one of them
                    striped candy canes they hang
                              from trees.

     And there he lie—
     just like I've seen him my whole life
                    in that dank garage
                    hot as hell
                    smelling like piss
               with his pants all half off his ass and
          that old broken toothpick clinging
                         to the back of his ear—
     something busted about him, man,

always something busted,
                    this time for good.

And I wish it was me
          cuz my life ain't worth a spit
          to the gutter, and mom says,
          I better run,
          better get out—
                    cuz they know you did it
                    and even if you didn't do it
                    why they gonna believe you?

     With tracks all up and down that
                    valley of arm,
                         looking like blueberries
                    busted all underneath the skin
                    They gonna say—
                         what's another injun strung
                              at the tip of Custer's prick,
                                   they gonna say.

And here I sit,
in this obscure motel thinking back
to the times when me and cousin Tee used to throw
rocks at the Sante Fe trains that would drag on
past the clubhouses we'd build from orange crates
talkin' about
     Shit, man!
     One day man I'm gonna be the conductor,
     that's right, I'm gonna wear them striped cap and overalls
     and I'm gonna pull on that horn so loud,
                              so loud,
     everyone's gonna know this train's coming!

But all of that seems pointless now,
here in this moment.
In this cheap-ass room with nothing
left to do except listen
to the distant ring of silence
and wonder why

Why the rhythm inside
my chest wants to beat me
                    senseless.

II.

Your father's death is only half
        the pain he's caused you, young man,

    The Judge explained to
C-Dog who sat slumped and
                hollow-eyed
        in the limp skin
                    of orange coveralls
                shackled in the accusing gate
                    of relatives
                        every exposed tattoo brimming now
                with a guilty luster
            exaggerated by the
                reflection from his clean-shaven head.

He showed no love!

            Tia Cuca shouted from the back row,
                her mascara running loose
                like bruises from the eyes—
                    wanting to scratch

her dead brother's nose
from her nephew's face

Wishing his high cheekbones
to drop
and his childish eyes
to lose
their glisten.

You don't deserve your father's name!

She roared.
C-Dog sobbing now
against the calluses that grew
from gripping bars &
balling up fists
in bunker brawls.
Tears leaking between each finger,
splashing on the tips of his state-issued sneakers,
some puddling on the cold courtroom floor,
others just drowning his eyes.

I heard them fighting, but that was no reason to go out there.

His mother spoke, growing fragile
in the lithe wings
of her black *rebozo,*
coughing, churning up phlegm,
excusing herself
—the death taking its toll
forcing C-Dog to remember;

The lucid hands of his father's ghost
still throttling at her thin neck,
striving to yank her tongue out

and pop the lungs like bubbles
the way he did every 1st and 15th of the month
when the check's arrival was reason enough
to shower, comb pomade through
the sideburns and two-step
to Club Intimo where *cochinos*
brooded over busty women
with jagged brows, bleached hair,
and long asses squeezing out
like *masa* from under sequin *faldas.*
Both boots teetering on the heels
he'd do the Wild Turkey shuffle
up the alley
through the front door
and into the kitchen
where he'd sharpen his claws
against the hard of her back.
Until one night C-Dog stumbled in
begging him to stop
and when his voice gave out
he gestured with a broomstick
managing to sweep the chaos
from his mother
onto himself.

The jury took notes:

Senseless
Peaches
Broomstick
Father's name
Intimo
Innocence

LONELY'S LONG BRONZE LEGS

sweep the winos, the lusters and
vagos of Chinatown
—but it's the vacancy of hips that gives her away.

Yesterday, she blew a *campesino*
behind the Kearny Fish Company.
While he closed his eyes and remembered a woman,

she spat his juice to the pavement like a hot cloud
unfurling over the city
    collected her pay

drew a crimson line around the edge of her lips
and strutted back
    into the sun's view of Fresno.

Yesterday, Lonely was the homeboy
    who stole roses from the courthouse garden
and pushed them on young men

sporting gold
machine gun medallions
at the swap mall

sucking sugar from *churro* sticks,
with chrome women
on their flat-bed
        pickups.

As a teenager,
Lonely grew to hate himself. In locker rooms,
where after gym the boys would shed their shorts

and expose their pale cheeks to one another,
he'd glance at their pink stiffies
from the corner of his eye and wonder why

his was smaller,
more shriveled,
        afraid.

Only time it grew into its skin
was at night,
when under the sheets he'd pinch it

and let it slide between his fingers,
    splendor at the sleek elasticity of it.
How one minute it was soft and bundled

and the next it grew hard and flexed at will.
He'd reach under the woolen mounds of hair,
        way beneath and find the place where it all began,

        the root, where it sprouted,
and with both fingers he'd press the base and discover
that it was, in fact, much longer than it revealed.

Lonely was afraid of being called a *maricon*.
        About becoming the barrio queer,
        the *comadres'* dream *chisme*,

about his dick falling off
and the children playing keep-away with his balls,
making up rhymes like:
                Lonely, Lonely, no balls and macaroni!!!

This is how it all began
The source of her secret
This is the city of her rabid solicitations

The cracked barrel of her double heart
These are the myths,
                    crippled as they appear.

First the face
made up in gutter sperm
        The rouge blush of night blood debtors

then the skirt,
curling its lip affectionately
                the moustache
                burns
                then the legs get waxed
                            until the sheen glows
                nose to the toes
                        bro!

ENTER MADRUGADA

with loose pants and leather sandals
a wide-brimmed hat with a black band

and lipstick on your deep cherry *guayabera*.
You staggered with a swagger into morning

remembering all the lines you fed the sequin-clad *mujer*
of yesterday's *tardeada,* who you flirted with and tried

to kiss until she laughed at you because she knew you
had a wife, six kids, a garden, and
an empty dog house.

So, you requested a song by Little Joe hoping he could take you
back to *Tejas* and all of this would be drunken hallucination.

When the accordion kicked in you jerked your hips like a teenager
at prom, trying to impress all the *viejas* with your timeless rhythm

but it didn't work—at first.
As the night crept you insisted on gambling your paycheck

and bought margaritas for every woman that approached
the bar, hoping it would be enough to fire up conversation,

until finally it was. Her name—you immediately forgot after
the introduction but it didn't matter because she spoke to you

like a true *Tejana* and that was enough reason to slow dance
the night away. When your zipper burned,

she knew what this would come down to, you both did.
After all the touching and breathing and moving in sync

After all the heat and sweat and exhaustion
After all the liquor and adrenaline, and your maleness
and her femininity

After all the lights expired and music retired,
the only thing left for chance was a small
thanks-for-everything kiss on the neck, which you
kindly accepted.

Enter *madrugada.*

Enter with *nopales, tomate, cebolla, y chile*
Enter with *familia.* A wife, a garden, and
an empty dog house

dreams of *Tejas* and a loose wallet,
now enter with lipstick on your deep cherry
guayabera.

For Felix Hernandez, Sr.

PERCHED ON THE FACE

      of a moon in a 1949 photograph
is how you'll exist in this poem.
The faded image of your tight blouse and
bobby-sox glee framed in billowing tendrils

      black as licorice
did no favors for your heart. It wasn't that the radio
dedicated slow songs to young lovers split by war,
or that the man you romanced called a flat-bed pickup

      home.
Not even the sweetness of your cherry lip-gloss
could save you from the tired gray of this photo,
much less from the worn back of the fieldhand's fate.

      It wasn't that South Texas
hated your skin and called you a Greaser because
your hands by age ten were thick enough to withstand
the sting of a ruler, and dark enough to

      neglect the bruises.
It wasn't because he promised you lush acreage
tucked amidst infinite landscapes, solid work loads
and sunsets, with brilliant stars to silhouette
the dreams,

      that made peculiar nights seem less
of an affair than his moustache would conceal.
Not even when you delicately brushed your lashes in
long strokes, pinched your cheeks to a warm fluster,

and dabbed rosemary on the bed of your wrists, did
you discover a breath to call your own.

  It was when the photographer flirted,
focused his lens, gently draped a black cloth over his eyes,
then asked you to smile—and you never stopped.

For Estela Constante

MADNESS FLOWS THROUGH

the house of Summer
when bed sheets are peeled from moist backs and
your lover's hand is an accomplice to the night

but even her hand isn't as guilty
as her hair with its wet gossamer of disgust
pillowing puddles of sea salt & sweat

When the painful memory of frostbite is
forgiven by the toes bones and
every joint grows stiff with nostalgia

when Santa Ana winds come cascading in
through screen doors, rapping
their knuckles fierce against kitchen windows

tonguing the backs of necks like
popsicle sticks sticky with
the sweetness of July's fever and

every walnut tree, blade of bluegrass, and
cluster of anise surrenders to the
radiant tint of yellow that permeates, then finally

your body gasps a reservoir of tears
until the ice cream truck comes
sliding up the block out of control in a

sherbet drool of orange-vanilla
and the only thing left to
keep the little ones from cringing

themselves into raisins is
a warm bowl
of watermelon cubes.

WHEN THE SKY SPILLS FORTH

like a hemorrhaging rainbow, festooned above the desert in the
skin of a cartoon, I think of you Mama. The alley you escaped to
when as a child you searched for a place to kneel, close your eyes
and wish apparitions of your mother against the back of trash cans,
or somewhere in the sky, beyond Akila, where you pumped gas and
tended to the reptiles while other girls hand jived and rumored away
their virginity.

This is where you gathered the kids, three girls / two boys, linked
fingers and rushed into the open sand, where against the barbed
teeth of tumbleweed and forgiving arms of *saguaros,* you whisper
sang lullabies to erase the air from its angry breath and your father's
shotgun that blasted shimmering holes into the night.

It was said, when he lost his harmonica, he quit jigging and
jitterbugging until his back arched and his eyebrows hung like black
veils with the memory of Korea and his dead wife. Shrapnel under
the skin. This is how he grew to resent. Erasing Deming with
war gin & a double-barrel incision. Until the last of his days crammed
themselves into a briefcase, still shot with memories
worn in gray.

I'M GONNA PUT VIRGIL DOWN

right here on this cloud
in front of you
so that you can't mistake him
for another brother

with his mama's curls
   sloven in iguana-skin belt
Alacran guero
   in the buckle,

   a white stinger for protection.
I'm gonna howl his howl
against the emptiness of this page
so that you don't mistake the monsoon

of his black luck for
another lowlife passing in the night.
Listen
   Hear the dying orphan inside?

The warrior voice of abandonment?
The slipping sand from his work boot?
Listen again

to the hot-rod temper
A hot spring spraying hot spit
from beneath the sallow
hardpan of a forty-year drought

Hear the man
   clank hammers?

Listen to his heave ho!
Hear it?

This is Virgil
Leather-necked Foreman
  of American 'hoods
  King of the desert

Of wrought iron &
              crumbling highways
Of enchanted lands &
              poisonous addictions

This is how he dances
when he is right;
    El Gusano
The drunken worm of *agave*

with lime in the cut
  clap / clap
the restless eyes shut
See him move, stroll

When he is wrong
the dance is visceral
His guts rumble, the heart plucks the ribcage
    A throbbing liver keeps tempo

Look—
You can see black musical notes
              slipping from the scars
A sonata of lonesome odes fluttering
about the fists

Tattoos bouncing from the skin
    A birthmark hangs on
    at the temple

Watch out!
    This is Virgil
    Father of prison guards &
                fleeting children

A moustache of stars
guards the stiffened lip of his jaw
where secrets are locked
    and romance tumbles

For the women who kept him—
there were greased engines,
    rigged pipes,
    polaroids,
    postcards of saints,
        and prayers

In the glove compartment
        letters of love
    & promises

A nicked ring
A dollar bill ripped in two
A million unlabeled keys
       & somewhere
       a million doors waiting to be opened.

This is Virgil
    in a box
    feeding himself to the earth

El Gusano
gobbled by a raven
that swoops from a corn husk
watered by the cloud
I'm puttin' him down on

So that you can't mistake him
for another brother
      in a poem.

"If you are a poet, then you will see clearly that there
is a cloud floating in this sheet of paper."
          —Thich Nhat Hanh

MAMA SPEAKS OF IT

Here, she pointed,
  is the incision see?

Mama shuttered
  at the sight of it.

Her eyes flexed
  and hung desperate.

Ever imagine a
  threaded breast

could look like
  a baseball mitt?

She joked. No more
  big catches to speak of

—no more games.

WHEN YOUNG ANDRES

      died before his book came out
not a poet in town could find the words.
Tongues hung

out to dry like crippled raisins
Out like burning flags
        gagging tears of ash

fire & smoke
weeping smudge stacks in big sky black
holding hands

in the cavity of church
where we gathered for the juice
like fire ants on a gutted grape.

      His voice tilling
tender and desperate at every reading,
praying poets find pulp in poems

When he sang/when he loved/
when he cried a verse to *God!*
      in the University Pit

books clapped shut
ravens jutted from tree limbs
        and rooftops

eyes yanked from lover's gaits
    students snapped pencils
smeared ink, blinked and listened.

In fertile soil
amidst bone orchards, blood dust,
and sweat, where crows clamor and swarm

up in clouds,
where summer ghosts rise from asphalt
    off the 99—

I imagine your voice, Andres
   in the warm baritone of earth,
reciting iceworker hymns

to seedlings not yet touching sky
lulling the roots of trees: peaches, plums, and figs
that will one day ripen to a plump sweetness

nourishing this hunger—
The fruit of our lives
                        as you've known it.

For Phil Goldvarg

IF I COULD TELL YOU

about the loss
　　　I've suffered in the bearing
month of May

　About the orchid blown
　from its supple root or
　　　how the calla lily cracked its bell

then you would see clearly
　　　that death & a cherry blossom
are of the same seed

　　and that a garden smiles
　with the brilliant teeth of hunger
　　and that my sadness isn't sadness at all

but a prayer for the passing
　A peach blossom to a peach
　　A fallen plum

bursting crimson from the bruised skin
　　　of its cheek
　　A cactus flower leaning

against the joy of daybreak
　　　And maybe then you would not forget
　that somewhere in the glorious

luster of birth
　there are petals opening
　　　to close as if by magic

And if you did not catch them
        if you did not bury your nose against their belly
    then you will not hear

            how they are mapping out
        your body when it rests
    when it touches ground

                again.